how2become

Scottish Police Tests
Numbers

www.How2Become.com

by How2become

Get more products for passing Scottish Police selection at:

www.How2Become.com

Orders: Please contact How2become Ltd, Suite 1, 60 Churchill Square Business Centre, Kings Hill, Kent ME19 4YU. You can also order via the email address info@how2become.co.uk

ISBN: 9781912370504

First published in 2018 by How2Become Ltd

Copyright © 2018 How2Become.

2nd Edition

Typeset for How2Become Ltd by Anton Pshinka.

CONTENT

As part of this product you have received FREE access to online tests that will help you to pass the Scottish Police Tests!

To gain access, simply go to:

www.PsychometricTestsOnline.co.uk

INTRODUCTION TO YOUR NEW GUIDE

Welcome to *Scottish Police Tests: Numbers Test*. This truly is the ULTIMATE guide for helping you to pass the standard mathematical entrance test, for the Scottish Police service!

The selection process to join Police Scotland is highly competitive. Approximately 65,000 people apply to join the police every year. But what is even more staggering is that only approximately 7,000 of those applicants will be successful. You could view this as a worrying statistic, or alternatively you could view it that you are determined to be one of the 7,000 who are successful. Armed with this insider's guide, you have certainly taken the first step to passing the Police Scotland selection process. There are plenty of test questions for you to try out within this guide which are relevant to the numbers test element of the selection process. Once you have completed the testing booklet you may wish to access our online police testing facility, which you can find at:

www.How2Become.com

Don't ever give up on your dreams; if you really want to become a Scottish police officer, then you can do it. The way to approach the police officer selection process is to embark on a programme of 'in-depth' preparation and this guide will help you to do exactly that. The police officer selection process is not easy to pass. Unless, that is, you put in plenty of preparation. Your preparation must be focused in the right areas, and also be comprehensive enough to give you every chance of success. In this book, we'll help you to prepare!

About the Scottish Police Standard Entrance Test

The test is made up of three papers. There are three different versions of the test, therefore all applicants are allowed to sit the Standard Entrance Test (SET) a maximum of three times. The test covers:

- Language;
- Numbers;
- Information Handling.

In this book we will be covering the Scottish Police **Numbers** Test.

You are allowed to use a calculator for this assessment. However, for the purposes of this book, we strongly encourage you to avoid using a calculator for the simpler questions. This will help you to think mathematically, and will make the other questions easier.

To help you get ready for the test, we've created sample numbers test questions for you to practice. Work through each test carefully before checking your answers at the end of the test. If you need any further help with any element of the police officer selection process, including role play, written test and interview, then we offer a wide range of products to assist you. These are all available through our online shop **www.How2Become.com.** We also run a 1-day intensive Police Officer Course.

Details are available at the website:

www.PoliceCourse.co.uk

Once again, thank you for your custom and we wish you every success in your pursuit to becoming a police officer.

Work hard, stay focused, and secure your dream career!

Best wishes,

The How2become Team

100 WARM-UP QUESTIONS

100 WARM-UP QUESTIONS

Within this first test there are 100 sample warm-up questions to get you prepared for the test exercises that follow. There is no time limit for this particular test.

1. 18 + 26

Answer [ ]

2. 97 − 46

Answer [ ]

3. 12 × 64

Answer [ ]

4. 5 × (12 × 11)

Answer [ ]

5. 74 ÷ 4

Answer [ ]

6. 4 × (4 + 5)

Answer [ ]

7. 11 × (4 + 5)

Answer

8. 80 ÷ 5

Answer

9. 4 × 4 × 6

Answer

10. 8 × (8 - 6)

Answer

11. 12 ÷ 4 × 6

Answer

12. 100 ÷ (4 + 1)

Answer

13. 216 − 158

Answer

14. 196 + 658

Answer

15. 856 ÷ 2

Answer

16. (4 × 4) + (5 × 6)

Answer

17. (4 + 6) × (12 − 6)

Answer

18. 30 ÷ 2 ÷ 3

Answer

19. 2 × 3 × 4

Answer

20. 146 ÷ 2

Answer

21. 123×3

Answer [   ]

22. $72 \div (8 + 10)$

Answer [   ]

23. $1,234 \times 4$

Answer [   ]

24. $453 + 1,987$

Answer [   ]

25. 45×46

Answer [   ]

26. $182 + 4 \times 2$

Answer [   ]

27. $9,753 - 679$

Answer [   ]

28. 7,547 − 975

Answer [   ]

29. 380 × 60

Answer [   ]

30. (6 × 12) × (8 × 15)

Answer [   ]

31. 12 × 123

Answer [   ]

32. 5,589 + 3,797

Answer [   ]

33. 35 × 235 − 17

Answer [   ]

34. (36 ÷ 3) + 58

Answer [   ]

35. 864 × 468

Answer [ ]

36. 985 ÷ 5

Answer [ ]

37. (78 ÷ 2) × 13

Answer [ ]

38. (46 × 12) × 4

Answer [ ]

39. 4 × (108 − 76)

Answer [ ]

40. (45 + 75) − 14

Answer [ ]

41. (49 − 38) × (13 + 12)

Answer [ ]

42. $690 \div 5 \times 2$

Answer [   ]

43. $876 \div 2 + 4$

Answer [   ]

44. 76×97

Answer [   ]

45. 863×10

Answer [   ]

46. $9,856 - 8,753$

Answer [   ]

47. $7,854 - 975$

Answer [   ]

48. $2 \times (6,035 + 204)$

Answer [   ]

49. 58 × 29

Answer [   ]

50. 12 × (4 + 6)

Answer [   ]

51. (873 − 3) − (456 − 123)

Answer [   ]

52. 30 × (150 ÷ 10)

Answer [   ]

53. (120 × 12) − (10 × 2)

Answer [   ]

54. 2,435 + 38

Answer [   ]

55. 9,786 − 134

Answer [   ]

56. 2,804 – 2,467

Answer [   ]

57. 60 × (4 × 4)

Answer [   ]

58. (9 × 8) ÷ 12

Answer [   ]

59. 2 × (6 × 12) + 3 × (4 + 7)

Answer [   ]

60. 986 ÷ 2

Answer [   ]

61. 23 × (57 + 93)

Answer [   ]

62. 12 × 5 × 6

Answer [   ]

63. 4,793 − 1,037 + 837

Answer [   ]

64. (10 × 6) ÷ 3

Answer [   ]

65. 8,276 − 1,256

Answer [   ]

66. 8,463 + 2,480

Answer [   ]

67. 8,436 − 8,406 ÷ 2

Answer [   ]

68. 349 × 87

Answer [   ]

69. 984 ÷ 6

Answer [   ]

70. 2,379 + 238

Answer [   ]

71. 12 × (502 + 38)

Answer [   ]

72. 39 × (93 - 87)

Answer [   ]

73. 3,498 – 2,002

Answer [   ]

74. (19 × 38) + (13 × 4)

Answer [   ]

75. 58 × 3

Answer [   ]

76. 974 × 4

Answer [   ]

77. 840 ÷ 4

Answer [ ]

78. 431 × 30

Answer [ ]

79. 34 × 97

Answer [ ]

80. 984 – 94

Answer [ ]

81. (83 - 71) + (38 × 3)

Answer [ ]

82. 2,379 – 100 + 345

Answer [ ]

83. 2 × (50 × 4) + 4 × (4 - 2)

Answer [ ]

84. 34 − 30 × 6

Answer [   ]

85. 23 × (90 ÷ 5)

Answer [   ]

86. 8,916 + 9,383

Answer [   ]

87. 120 × 432

Answer [   ]

88. 900 ÷ 12

Answer [   ]

89. (23 × 6) − (12 - 3)

Answer [   ]

90. 124 − 93

Answer [   ]

91. 973 + 804

Answer

92. 2 × (83 + 27) + 3 × (5 × 6)

Answer

93. 8,542 − 1,267

Answer

94. 36 ÷ (12 - 6)

Answer

95. 40 ÷ (5 × 2)

Answer

96. 235 × 125

Answer

97. 884 ÷ 4

Answer

98. $2,367 \times 23$

Answer [   ]

99. 64×34

Answer [   ]

100. $(23 \times 34) + (34 \times 12)$

Answer [   ]

ANSWERS TO 100 WARM-UP QUESTIONS

1. 44

EXPLANATION = 18 + 26 = 44

2. 51

EXPLANATION = 97 − 46 = 51

3. 768

EXPLANATION = 12 × 64 = 768

4. 660

EXPLANATION = 12 × 11 = 132. 5 × 132 = 660

5. 18.5

EXPLANATION = 74 ÷ 4 = 18.5

6. 36

EXPLANATION = 4 + 5 = 9. 4 × 9 = 36

7. 99

EXPLANATION = 4 + 5 = 9. 11 × 9 = 99

8. 16

EXPLANATION = 80 ÷ 5 = 16

9. 96

EXPLANATION = 4 × 4 = 16. 16 × 6 = 96

10. 16

EXPLANATION = 8 − 6 = 2. 2 × 8 = 16

11. 18

EXPLANATION = 12 ÷ 4 = 3. 3 × 6 = 18

12. 20

EXPLANATION = $4 + 1 = 5$. $100 \div 5 = 20$

13. 58

EXPLANATION = $216 - 158 = 58$

14. 854

EXPLANATION = $196 + 658 = 854$

15. 428

EXPLANATION = $856 \div 2 = 428$

16. 46

EXPLANATION = $4 \times 4 = 16$. $5 \times 6 = 30$. $30 + 16 = 46$

17. 60

EXPLANATION = $4 + 6 = 10$. $12 - 6 = 6$. $10 \times 6 = 60$

18. 5

EXPLANATION = $30 \div 2 = 15$. $15 \div 3 = 5$

19. 24

EXPLANATION = $2 \times 3 = 6$. $6 \times 4 = 24$

20. 73

EXPLANATION = $146 \div 2 = 73$

21. 369

EXPLANATION = $123 \times 3 = 369$

22. 4

EXPLANATION = $8 + 10 = 18$. $72 \div 18 = 4$

23. 4,936

EXPLANATION = $1234 \times 4 = 4,936$

24. 2,440

EXPLANATION = 453 + 1987 = 2,440

25. 2,070

EXPLANATION = 45 × 46 = 2,070

26. 190

EXPLANATION = 4 × 2 = 8. 182 + 8 = 190

27. 9,074

EXPLANATION = 9,753 − 679 = 9,074

28. 6,572

EXPLANATION = 7,547 − 975 = 6,572

29. 22,800

EXPLANATION = 380 × 60 = 22,800

30. 8,640

EXPLANATION = 6 × 12 = 72. 8 × 15 = 120. 120 × 72 = 8,640

31. 1,476

EXPLANATION = 12 × 123 = 1,476

32. 9,386

EXPLANATION = 5,589 + 3,797 = 9,386

33. 8,208

EXPLANATION = 35 × 235 = 8,225. 8,225 − 17 = 8,208

34. 70

EXPLANATION = 36 ÷ 3 = 12. 12 + 58 = 70

35. 404,352

EXPLANATION = 864 × 468 = 404,352

36. 197

EXPLANATION = $985 \div 5 = 197$

37. 507

EXPLANATION = $78 \div 2 = 39$. $39 \times 13 = 507$

38. 2,208

EXPLANATION = $46 \times 12 = 552$. $552 \times 4 = 2,208$

39. 128

EXPLANATION = $108 - 76 = 32$. $32 \times 4 = 128$

40. 106

EXPLANATION = $45 + 75 = 120$. $120 - 14 = 106$

41. 275

EXPLANATION = $49 - 38 = 11$. $13 + 12 = 25$. $11 \times 25 = 275$

42. 276

EXPLANATION = $690 \div 5 = 138$. $138 \times 2 = 276$

43. 442

EXPLANATION = $876 \div 2 = 438$. $438 + 4 = 442$

44. 7,372

EXPLANATION = $76 \times 97 = 7,372$

45. 8,630

EXPLANATION = $863 \times 10 = 8,630$

46. 1,103

EXPLANATION = $9,856 - 8,753 = 1,103$

47. 6,879

EXPLANATION = $7,854 - 975 = 6,879$

48. 12,478

EXPLANATION = 6,035 + 204 = 6,239. 6,239 × 2 = 12,478

49. 1,682

EXPLANATION = 58 × 29 = 1,682

50. 120

EXPLANATION = 4 + 6 = 10. 10 × 12 = 120

51. 537

EXPLANATION = 873 − 3 = 870. 456 − 123 = 333. 870 − 333 = 537

52. 450

EXPLANATION = 150 ÷ 10 = 15. 30 × 15 = 450

53. 1,420

EXPLANATION = 120 × 12 = 1,440. 10 × 2 = 20. 1,440 − 20 = 1,420

54. 2,473

EXPLANATION = 2,435 + 38 = 2,473

55. 9,652

EXPLANATION = 9,786 − 134 = 9,652

56. 337

EXPLANATION = 2804 − 2467 = 337

57. 960

EXPLANATION = 16 × 60 = 960

58. 6

EXPLANATION = 9 × 8 = 72. 72 ÷ 12 = 6

59. 177

EXPLANATION = 6 × 12 = 72. 72 × 2 = 144
4 + 7 = 11. 3 × 11 = 33.
144 + 33 = 177

60. 493

EXPLANATION = 986 ÷ 2 = 493

61. 3,450

EXPLANATION = 57 + 93 = 150. 150 × 23 = 3,450

62. 360

EXPLANATION = 12 × 5 = 60. 60 × 6 = 360

63. 4,593

EXPLANATION = 4,793 − 1037 = 3756. 3,756 + 837 = 4,593

64. 20

EXPLANATION = 10 × 6 = 60. 60 ÷ 3 = 20

65. 7,020

EXPLANATION = 8,276 − 1,256 = 7,020

66. 10,943

EXPLANATION = 8,463 + 2,480 = 10,943

67. 4,233

EXPLANATION = 8,406 ÷ 2 = 4,203. 8,436 − 4,203 = 4,233

68. 30,363

EXPLANATION = 349 × 87 = 30,363

69. 164

EXPLANATION = 984 ÷ 6 = 164

70. 2,617

EXPLANATION = 2,379 + 238 = 2,617

71. 6,480

EXPLANATION = 502 + 38 = 540. 540 × 12 = 6,480

72. 234

EXPLANATION = 93 − 87 = 6. 6 × 39 = 234

73. 1,496

EXPLANATION = 3,498 − 2,002 = 1,496

74. 774

EXPLANATION = 19 × 38 = 722. 13 × 4 = 52. 722 + 52 = 774

75. 174

EXPLANATION = 58 × 3 = 174

76. 3,896

EXPLANATION = 974 × 4 = 3,896

77. 210

EXPLANATION = 840 ÷ 4 = 210

78. 12,930

EXPLANATION = 431 × 30 = 12,930

79. 3,298

EXPLANATION = 34 × 97 = 3,298

80. 890

EXPLANATION = 984 − 94 = 890

81. 126

EXPLANATION = 12 + 114 = 126

82. 2,624

EXPLANATION = 2,379 − 100 = 2,279. 2,279 + 345 = 2,624

83. 408

EXPLANATION = 50 × 4 = 200. 200 × 2 = 400.
4 − 2 = 2. 4 × 2 = 8.
400 + 8 = 408.

84. -146

EXPLANATION = 30 × 6 = 180. 34 − 180 = -146

85. 414

EXPLANATION = 90 ÷ 5 = 18. 18 × 23 = 414

86. 18,299

EXPLANATION = 8,916 + 9,383 = 18,299

87. 51,840

EXPLANATION = 120 × 432 = 51,840

88. 75

EXPLANATION = 900 ÷ 12 = 75

89. 129

EXPLANATION = 23 × 6 = 138. 12 − 3 = 9. 138 − 9 = 129

90. 31

EXPLANATION = 124 − 93 = 31

91. 1,777

EXPLANATION = 973 + 804 = 1,777

92. 310

EXPLANATION = 83 + 27 = 110. 2 × 110 = 220
5 × 6 = 30. 3 × 30 = 90
220 + 90 = 310

93. 7,275

EXPLANATION = 8,542 − 1,267 = 7,275

94. 6

EXPLANATION = 12 − 6 = 6. 36 ÷ 6 = 6

95. 4

EXPLANATION = 5 × 2 = 10. 40 ÷ 10 = 4

96. 29,375

EXPLANATION = 235 × 125 = 29,375

97. 221

EXPLANATION = 884 ÷ 4 = 221

98. 54,441

EXPLANATION = 2,367 × 23 = 54,441

99. 2,176

EXPLANATION = 64 × 34 = 2,176

100. 1,190

EXPLANATION = 23 × 34 = 782. 34 × 12 = 408. 782 + 408 = 1,190

Congratulations on completing the warm-up questions. Now move onto the timed numbers exercises contained within the remainder of your guide.

NUMBERS EXERCISE 1

NUMBERS EXERCISE 1

Try to answer the questions quickly. You have 5 minutes in which to answer the 14 questions.

1. A wallet has been found containing one £20 note, five £5 notes, a fifty pence coin and three 2 pence coins. How much is in the wallet?

Answer [ ]

2. Subtract 200 from 500, add 80, subtract 30 and multiply by 2. What number do you have?

Answer [ ]

3. A multi-storey car park has 8 floors and can hold 72 cars on each floor. In addition to this, there are 4 allocated disabled parking spaces per floor. How many spaces are there in the entire car park?

Answer [ ]

4. A man saves £12.50 per month. How much would he have saved after 1 year?

Answer [ ]

5. If there have been 60 accidents along one stretch of a motorway in the last year, how many on average have occurred each month?

Answer [ ]

6. Out of 40,000 applicants only 4,000 are likely to be successful. What percentage will fail?

Answer [   ]

7. What percentage of 400 is 100?

Answer [   ]

8. Malcolm's shift commences at 0615 hours. If his shift is 10.5 hours long what time will he finish?

Answer [   ]

9. If Mary can bake 12 cakes in 2 hours, how many will she bake in 10 hours?

Answer [   ]

10. If there are 24 hours in the day, how many hours are there in one week?

Answer [   ]

11. Susan has 10 coins and gives 5 of them to Steven and the remainder to Alan. Alan gives 3 of his coins to Steven who in turn gives half of his back to Susan. How many is Susan left with?

Answer [   ]

12. Add 121 to 54. Now subtract 75 and multiply by 10. What is the result?

Answer [   ]

13. Ahmed leaves for work at 8am and arrives at work at 9.17am. He then leaves work at 4.57pm and arrives back at home at 6.03pm. How many minutes has Ahmed spent travelling?

Answer [ ]

14. A car travels at 30 km/h for the first hour, 65km/h for the second hour, 44 km/h for the third hour and 50 km/h for the fourth hour. What is the car's average speed over the 4-hour journey?

Answer [ ]

ANSWERS TO NUMBERS EXERCISE 1

For this section, we have provided you detailed explanations to show you how to work out the answers.

1. £45.56

EXPLANATION = 20.00 + 5.00 + 5.00 + 5.00 + 5.00 + 5.00 + 0.50 + 0.02 + 0.02 + 0.02 = £45.56

2. 700

EXPLANATION = 500 − 200 = 300

300 + 80 − 30 = 350 × 2 = 700

3. 608

EXPLANATION = (8 × 72) + (4 × 8) = 576 + 32 = 608

4. £150

EXPLANATION = 12.50 × 12 = £150

5. 5

EXPLANATION = 60 ÷ 12 = 5

6. 90%

EXPLANATION = Out of 40,000 applicants, 36,000 people will fail. 10% of 40,000 = 4,000.

36,000 ÷ 4,000 = 9% × 10 = 90% of people will fail.

7. 25%

EXPLANATION = 100 is 25% of 400.

8. 1645 hours or 4.45pm

EXPLANATION = You need to add 10 hours and 30 minutes to 0615 which gives you the answer of 4.45 pm.

9. 60 cakes

EXPLANATION = If Mary can bake 12 cakes in 2 hours, in 10 hours, she will be able to make 60.

12 × 5 = 60

10. 168

EXPLANATION = 24 × 7 = 168 hours

11. 4

EXPLANATION = Susan has 10 coins and gives 5 to Stephen – Stephen now has 5. She gives the remainder to Alan, so now Alan has 5, but he gives three of them to Stephen – Stephen now has 8. He gives half of them back to Susan, so Susan now has 4.

12. 1,000

EXPLANATION = 121 + 54 = 175

175 – 75 = 100 × 10 = 1,000

13. 143 minutes

EXPLANATION = 8 am to 9.17 am = 1 hour and 17 minutes (77 minutes)

4.57 pm to 6:03 pm = 1 hour and 6 minutes (66 minutes)

77 + 66 = 143 minutes

14. 47.25 km/h

EXPLANATION = 30 + 65 + 44 + 50 = 189

189 divided by 4 hours = 47.25

NUMBERS EXERCISE 2

NUMBERS EXERCISE 2

You are permitted to use a calculator during this exercise.
You have 10 minutes in which to answer 20 multiple-choice questions.

1. Your friends tell you their electricity bill has gone up from £40 per month to £47 per month. How much extra are they now paying per year?

a. £84 b. £85 c. £83 d. £86 e. £82

Answer [   ]

2. A woman earns a salary of £32,000 per year. How much would she earn in 15 years?

a. £280,000 b. £380,000 c. £480,000 d. £260,000 e. £460,000

Answer [   ]

3. If a police officer walks the beat for 6 hours at a pace of 4km/h, how much ground will she have covered after the 6 hours is over?

a. 20km b. 21km c. 22km d. 23km e. 24km

Answer [   ]

4. It takes Malcolm 45 minutes to walk 6 miles to work. At what pace does he walk?

a. 7 mph b. 4 mph c. 6 mph d. 5 mph e. 8 mph

Answer [   ]

5. Ellie spends 3 hours on the phone talking to her friend abroad. If the call costs 12 pence per 5 minutes, how much does the call cost in total?

a. £3.30 b. £4.32 c. £3.32 d. £4.44 e. £3.44

Answer [   ]

6. A woman spends £27 in a retail store. She has a discount voucher that reduces the total cost to £21.60. How much discount does the voucher give her?

a. 5%   b. 10%   c. 15%   d. 20%   e. 25%

Answer [   ]

7. A group of 7 men spend £21.70 on a round of drinks. How much does each of them pay if the bill is split evenly?

a. £3.00   b. £65.10   c. £3.10   d. £3.15   e. £3.20

Answer [   ]

8. 45,600 people attend a football match to watch North Ficshire play South Ficshire. If there are 32,705 North Ficshire supporters at the game, how many South Ficshire supporters are there?

a. 12,985   b. 13,985   c. 12,765   d. 12,895   e. 14,985

Answer [   ]

9. The police are called to attend a motorway accident involving a coach full of passengers. A total of 54 people are on board, 17 of whom are injured. How many are not injured?

a. 40   b. 39   c. 38   d. 37   e. 36

Answer [   ]

10. A car journey usually takes 6 hrs and 55 minutes, but on one occasion, the car also has to stop for an extra 47 minutes. How long does the journey take on this occasion?

a. 6 hrs 40 mins   b. 5 hrs 45 mins   c. 7 hrs 40 mins   d. 7 hrs 42 mins

e. 6 hrs 42 mins

Answer [   ]

11. There are 10 people in a team. Five of them weigh 70 kg each and the remaining 5 weigh 75 kg each. What is the average weight of the team?

a. 72.5 kg   b. 71.5 kg   c. 70.5 kg   d. 72 kg   e. 71 kg

Answer [   ]

12. A kitchen floor takes 80 tiles to cover. A man buys 10 boxes, each containing 6 tiles. How many more boxes does he need to complete the job?

a. 2 boxes   b. 4 boxes   c. 6 boxes   d. 8 boxes   e. 10 boxes

Answer [   ]

13. How much money does it cost to buy 12 packets of crisps at 47 pence each?

a. £6.45   b. £5.64   c. £6.54   d. £4.65   e. £5.46

Answer [   ]

14. A motorcyclist is travelling at 78 mph on a road where the speed limit is 50 mph. How much over the speed limit is he?

a. 20 mph   b. 22 mph   c. 26 mph   d. 28 mph   e. 30 mph

Answer [　　　　　　　　　]

15. A removal firm loads 34 boxes onto a van. If there are 27 boxes still to be loaded, how many boxes are there in total?

a. 49   b. 50   c. 61   d. 52   e. 53

Answer [　　　　　　　　　]

16. When paying a bill at the bank you give the cashier one £20 note, two £5 notes, four £1 coins, six 10p coins and two 2p coins. How much have you given him?

a. £34.64   b. £43.46   c. £34.46   d. £63.44   e. £36.46

Answer [　　　　　　　　　]

17. If you pay £97.70 per month on your council tax bill, how much would you pay quarterly?

a. £293.30   b. £293.20   c. £293.10   d. £293.00   e. £292.90

Answer [　　　　　　　　　]

18. Four people eat a meal at a restaurant. The total bill comes to £44.80. How much do they need to pay each?

a. £10.00   b. £10.10   c. £10.20   d. £11.10   e. £11.20

Answer [　　　　　　　　　]

19. Victor works between 8am and 4pm. He is entitled to three 20-minute breaks and one 1-hour lunch break during that 8-hour period. If he works for 5 days per week, how many hours will he have worked after 4 weeks?

a. 12 hours b. 14 hours c. 120 hours d. 140 hours e. 150 hours

Answer

20. If there are 610 metres in a mile, how many metres are there in 4 miles?

a. 240   b. 2,040   c. 2,044   d. 2,440   e. 244

Answer

ANSWERS TO NUMBERS EXERCISE 2

For this section, we have provided you detailed explanations to show you how to work out the answers.

1. a. £84

EXPLANATION = In this question you need to first work out the difference in their electricity bill. Subtract £40 from £47 to be left with £7. Now you need to calculate how much extra they are paying per year. If there are 12 months in a year then you need to multiply £7 by 12 months to reach your answer of £84.

2. c. £480,000

EXPLANATION = The lady earns £32,000 per year. To work out how much she earns in 15 years, you must multiply £32,000 by 15 years to reach your answer of £480,000.

3. e. 24km

EXPLANATION = To work this answer out all you need to do is multiply the 6 hours by the 4 km/h to reach the total of 24 km. Remember that she is walking at a pace of 4 km per hour for a total of 6 hours.

4. e. 8mph

EXPLANATION = Malcolm walks 6 miles in 45 minutes, which means he is walking two miles every 15 minutes. Therefore, he would walk 8 miles in 60 minutes (1 hour), so he is walking at 8 mph.

5. b. £4.32

EXPLANATION = If the call costs 12 pence for every 5 minutes, then all you need to do is calculate how many 5 minutes there are in the 3-hour telephone call. There are 60 minutes in every hour, so therefore there are 180 minutes in 3 hours. 180 minutes divided by 5 minutes will give you 36. To get your answer, just multiply 36 by 12 pence to reach your answer of £4.32

6. d. 20%

EXPLANATION = This type of question can be tricky. The best way to work out the answer is to first of all work out how much 10% discount would give you off the total price. If £27 is the total price, then 10% would be a £2.70 discount. In monetary terms, the woman has received £5.40 in discount. If 10% is a £2.70 discount, then 20% is a £5.40 discount.

7. c. £3.10

EXPLANATION = Divide £21.70 by 7 to reach your answer of £3.10.

8. d. 12,895

EXPLANATION = Subtract 32,705 from 45,600 to reach your answer of 12,895.

9. d. 37

EXPLANATION = Subtract 17 from 54 to reach your answer of 37.

10. d. 7 hrs 42 minutes

EXPLANATION = Add the 47 minutes to the normal journey time of 6 hrs and 55 minutes to reach your answer of 7 hrs and 42 minutes.

11. a. 72.5 kg

EXPLANATION = To calculate the average weight, you need to first of all add each weight together. Therefore, (5 x 70) + (5 x 75) = 725 kg. To find the average weight you must now divide the 725 by 10, which will give you the answer 72.5 kg.

12. b. 4 boxes

EXPLANATION = The man has 10 boxes, each of which contains 6 tiles. He therefore has a total of 60 tiles. He now needs a further 20 tiles to cover the total floor area. If there are 6 tiles in a box, then he will need a further 4 boxes (24 tiles).

13. b. £5.64

EXPLANATION = Multiply 12 by 47 pence to reach your answer of £5.64.

14. d. 28 mph

EXPLANATION = Subtract 50 mph from 78 mph to reach your answer of 28 mph.

15. c. 61

EXPLANATION = Add 34 to 27 to reach your answer of 61 boxes.

16. a. £34.64

EXPLANATION = Add all of the money together to reach the answer of £34.64.

17. c. £293.10

EXPLANATION = To reach the answer you must multiply £97.70 by 3. Remember, a quarter is every 3 months.

18. e. £11.20

EXPLANATION = Divide £44.80 by 4 people to reach your answer of £11.20.

19. c. 120 hours

EXPLANATION = First of all you need to determine how many 'real' hours he works each day. Subtract the total sum of breaks from 8 hours to reach 6 hours per day. If he works 5 days per week, then he is working a total of 30 hours per week. Multiply 30 hours by 4 weeks to reach your answer of 120 hours.

20. d. 2,440 metres

EXPLANATION = Multiply 4 by 610 metres to reach your answer of 2,440 metres.

NUMBERS EXERCISE 3

NUMBERS EXERCISE 3

Try to answer the questions quickly. You have 12 minutes in which to answer the 25 questions.

Q1. There are 400 cows in the barn. The ratio of cows to sheep, is 20:5. How many sheep are there?

Answer

Q2. Due to riots in the town of Ficshire, the western gate to the city was locked between the hours of 23:40 on Thursday, and 14:00 on Saturday. People were without food and water for a sustained period of time. How long was the western gate locked for? Give your answer in hours and minutes.

Answer

Q3. There are 2 circles, 1 triangle and a rhombus. How many individual 360 angles are there?

Answer

Q4. Martin ate dinner in his local restaurant. The restaurant charges on a time spent basis. The charge is £15.50 per hour. Martin spent 3 hours at the restaurant, before going home. How much did the restaurant charge Martin?

Answer

Q5. Daisy and Emily went on holiday to Barbados. They arrived on the 6th July, and left on the 8th August. How many days were they on holiday for?

Answer

Q6. A local running club charges £4 per adult to use the facilities, and £2 per child. On Sunday there were 18 adults who used the running club, and 3 children. How much money did the running club make on Sunday?

Answer [   ]

Q7. Miranda visits the supermarket every Monday. She needs £78.50 to cover the entire week's worth of food. On average, what is the value of food that Miranda consumes per day? Round your answer to the nearest pound.

Answer [   ]

Q8. A prison guard left the door open, and now 64% of the prisoners from Ficshire Security Centre have escaped. There are 1,568 prisoners left. How many prisoners were there originally?

Answer [   ]

Q9. Jason became ill on Monday. He went to bed on Monday night at 8pm, and then woke 14 hours later. What time did he wake up?

Answer [   ]

Q10. Elizabeth runs a day care service. She has 15 toys at her day care centre. Today, Elizabeth is looking after five children. She wants to give them some toys to play with, whilst she takes a nap. One of the toys is broken, so this cannot be given out.

The children are named Benjamin, Sarah, Janice, Pete and Wallace.

The ratio of toys being shared amongst the children is 1:5:6:1:1

How many toys did each child get?

Answer [   ]

Q11. A steel manufacturing company in the East of England has a staff leaving rate of 540 people per year. How many people, on average, left the company per month?

Answer [ ]

Q12. There are 600 points available in a video game. Tommy and Wayne agree that, to keep things fair, they will call it a draw and split the points equally. However, they also agree to give Vincent 1/5th of the points. How many points will Tommy and Wayne get?

Answer [ ]

13. Tom and Sarah went away on holiday for 5 weeks. How many days in total did they go away for?

Answer [ ]

14. Sandy drew 4 squares and 6 rectangles on a piece of paper. How many 90 degree angles were there?

Answer [ ]

15. Mandy has 3 dogs. She buys dog food every two weeks. She needs 1 tin of dog food per day, per dog. Each tin costs £1.20. How much does Mandy spend every two weeks on dog food?

Answer [ ]

16. David parked his car in a car park at 7:00 pm. The car park charges £5.50 per hour after 7:00 pm. David got back to his car at 11:00pm. How much does David have to pay?

Answer [   ]

17. Lucy bought 3 apples, 2 bananas and an orange. Each apple costs 55p, each banana costs 65p and each orange is 60p each. Lucy pays with a £10 note. How much change will she receive?

Answer [   ]

18. A salon charges £12.50 for gentleman's cuts and £25.00 for ladies cuts. One particular day the salon had 9 clients, 5 of which were male. How much money did the salon make that day?

Answer [   ]

19. A football stadium holds 45,000 spectators. 65% of the spectators were male. How many spectators were men?

Answer [   ]

20. A concert is expecting 26,000 people. The ratio of police needed for the concert would be 1:130 people. How many police would be needed for that night?

Answer [   ]

21. A child had £5.00 to spend in a sweet shop. She picked up a bag of crisps costing £1.20, a bottle of pop costing £0.60 and a bag of sweets costing £2.10. How much change would she receive?

Answer [   ]

22. Sam drew 5 equilateral triangles on a page. How many angles were 60 degrees?

Answer [   ]

23. An accident on the motorway occurred at 1300 hours. It took 5 hours for the police to open up the road. What time was traffic able to move again?

Answer [   ]

24. Heavy rain during the week resulted in a bridge being closed between the hours of 1445 and 1630 on Tuesday, 1125 and 1350 on Wednesday and 0700 and 1115 on Thursday. For how long (in hours and minutes) was the bridge closed altogether?

Answer [   ]

25. Mia and Richard went on holiday from January 1st to March 22nd. How many days did Mia and Richard have on holiday in total? (Count from the first day they left to the last day they were there.)

Answer [   ]

ANSWERS TO NUMBERS EXERCISE 3

1. 80

EXPLANATION = 400 / 25 = 16. 16 × 5 = 80. Therefore, there are 80 sheep.

2. 38 hours and 20 minutes

EXPLANATION = Answer: 38 hours and 20 minutes.

23:40 plus 20 minutes would give you 00:00 Friday. Plus 24 hours would give you 00:00 Saturday, plus 14 hours would give you 14:00 Saturday. Add the 24, plus the 14, plus the 20 minutes, and you get the answer.

3. 2

EXPLANATION = The two circles are the only shapes in the list with an individual 360 degree angle.

4. £46.50

EXPLANATION = Martin spent 3 hours at the restaurant, with each hour costing £15.50. £15.50 × 3 = £46.50

5. 33 days

EXPLANATION = From the 6th July till the 8th August = 33 days.

6. £78

EXPLANATION = £18 × 4 = £72. £2 × 3 = £6. £72 + £6 = £78

7. £11

EXPLANATION = Divide Miranda's weekly spend on a per-day basis, so £78.50 divided by 7 = £11

8. 2,450

EXPLANATION = 1,568 / 64 = 24.5, which = 1%. So 24.5 × 100 = 2,450.

9. Tuesday, 10am

EXPLANATION = Monday night 8pm + 14 hours = 10am Tuesday morning

10. Benjamin 1, Sarah 5, Janice 6, Pete 1, Wallace 1.

EXPLANATION = The ratio is already worked out for you, since the numbers given equal the amount of toys available.

11. 45 people per month

EXPLANATION = There are 12 months in a year. 540 people left in total during the year, so 540/12 gives you the average, which is 45.

12. 240 points each

EXPLANATION = There are 600 points total. If Tommy and Wayne give Vincent 1/5th of the points, there will be 480 points left, which means 240 points for Tommy and Wayne when split equally.

13. 35

EXPLANATION = 7 days in a week. 5 weeks = 35 days.

14. 40

EXPLANATION = 1 square = 4 right angles. 4 squares = 16 right angles. 1 rectangle = 4 right angles. 6 rectangles = 24 right angles.
16 + 24 = 40.

15. £50.40

EXPLANATION = £1.20 × 3 = daily spend of £3.60. 2 weeks = 14 days. £3.60 × 14 = £50.40.

16. £22.00

EXPLANATION = 7pm to 11pm = 4 hours. £5.50 × 4 = £22.

17. £6.45

EXPLANATION = 3 × £0.55 = £1.65
2 × £0.65 = £1.30

$1 \times £0.60 = £0.60$
$£1.65 + £1.30 + £0.60 = £3.55. £10 - £3.55 = £6.45$

18. £162.50

EXPLANATION = $£12.50 \times 5 = £62.50$
$£25 \times 4 = £100$
$£100 + £62.50 = £162.50.$

19. 29,250 male spectators

EXPLANATION = $65\% = 65 \div 100 = 0.65. 0.65 \times 45,000 = 29,250.$

20. 200 police needed

EXPLANATION = $26000 \div 130 = 200. 200 \times 1 = 200.$

21. £1.10

EXPLANATION = $£1.20 + £0.60 + £2.10 = £3.90. £5 - £3.90 = £1.10$

22. 15

EXPLANATION = 1 equilateral triangle = 3 angles of 60°. Therefore 5 equilateral triangles = 15 angles of 60°

23. 1800

EXPLANATION = 13:00 + 5 hours = 18:00

24. 8hrs and 25minutes

EXPLANATION = 14:45 to 16:30 = 1 hour and 45 minutes
11:25 to 13:50 = 2 hours and 25 minutes
07:00 to 11:15 = 4 hours and 15 minutes
When added together these times total 8 hours and 25 minutes.

25. 81 days

EXPLANATION = 31 days in January + 28 days in February + 22 days of March = 81 days total.

NUMBERS EXERCISE 4

NUMBERS EXERCISE 4

Try to answer the questions quickly. You have 12 minutes in which to answer the 25 questions.

1. Tommy carried out his weekly food shop, which came to £178.00 in total. If he used a 20% discount voucher at checkout, how much would he pay?

Answer

2. Jane wants to buy a dress that costs £20.00. If it was discounted by 15%, how much would Jane have to pay for the dress?

Answer

3. Michael paid £45.00 for 4 films. On average how much did he pay for each film?

Answer

4. A singing choir consists of 72 people. The male to female ratio of the choir is 2:6. How many people are male in the choir?

Answer

5. Elliott drew 12 squares and 3 rectangles on the computer. How many right angles are there?

Answer

6. A company employed 28,000 people in one particular year but they had to let go 25% of their employees. How many people did they have to let go of?

Answer

7. Rachel wanted to buy a top costing £17.50, a pair of trousers costing £12.50 and a jumper costing £9.00. Rachel would receive a 10% discount of the final cost. How much would Rachel have to pay?

Answer

8. A school play had an audience of 150 people. The ratio of grandparents to parents is 2:3. How many grandparents and how many parents were at the school play?

Answer

9. Peter buys 5 films costing £6.00 each and 3 books that cost £4.60 each. How much did Peter spend altogether?

Answer

10. A cruise ship would take 32 hours to reach its final destination. If the ship leaves on Monday at 1300 hours, what day would the ship arrive at its final destination?

Answer

11. Heavy snow during the week resulted in a countryside road being closed between the hours of 0845 and 1430 on Tuesday, 1125 and 1650 on Wednesday and 1600 and 2315 on Friday. For how long (in hours and minutes) was the road closed altogether?

Answer

12. A company employed 3,550 people in one particular year and 30% of staff received a bonus at the end of the year. How many employees received a bonus?

Answer

13. Tommy had 32 sweets. He had to share them equally between himself and 3 other people. How many sweets did they each receive?

Answer

14. Gareth had 4 yellow balls, 2 pink balls and 1 orange ball. What is the ratio?

Answer

15. Sandra bought 5 tops costing £70.50 in total. On average, how much was each top?

Answer

16. If Sammy drew 6 triangles, altogether how many degrees are there?

Answer

17. Alana had 100 pairs of shoes. She decided to get rid of a quarter of them. How many pairs of shoes does Alana have left?

Answer

18. A lady has 2 goats and 3 pigs. The cost of a bag of goat food is £23.50 and a bag of pig food costs £17.60. In a month, she needs 3 bags of goat food and 5 bags of pig food. How much money does the lady spend per month?

Answer

19. There are 45 men and 15 women in a pub. What is the ratio, in its simplest form, of males to females?

Answer

20. Elliott has 3 times more football trophies than Brad, who has 6 football trophies. How many football trophies does Elliott have?

Answer

21. A child goes in to a shop with a £10.00 note. He spends 10% of his money. How much money does the child have left?

Answer

22. Tom receives £560 a week. On average how much does Tom get per day?

Answer

23. There are 20 cats and 5 rabbits in a pet shelter. What is the ratio, in its simplest form, of cats to rabbits?

Answer [   ]

24. Billy has 500 × 1p coins and 100 × 2p coins. How much money does Billy have altogether?

Answer [   ]

25. Lucy works 20 hours a week and she gets paid £7 per hour. How much money does Lucy earn in 4 weeks?

Answer [   ]

ANSWERS TO NUMBERS EXERCISE 4

1. £142.40

EXPLANATION = 20% = 20 ÷ 100 = 0.20. 0.20 × £178 = £35.60. £178 − 35.60 = £142.40

2. £17.00

EXPLANATION = 15% = 15 ÷ 100 = 0.15. 0.15 × £20 = £3. £20 - £3 = £17.00

3. £11.25

EXPLANATION = £45.00 ÷ 4 = £11.25 on average per film.

4. 18

EXPLANATION = 2 + 6 = 8. 72 ÷ 8 = 9. 2 × 9 = 18, 6 × 9 = 52. 18 + 54 = 72, meaning there are 18 male members of the choir.

5. 60

EXPLANATION = 1 square = 4 right angles. Therefore 12 squares = 48 right angles.

1 rectangle = 4 right angles. Therefore 3 rectangles = 12 right angles.

48 + 12 = 60 right angles in total.

6. 7,000 people

EXPLANATION = 25% = 25 ÷ 100 = 0.25. 0.25 × 28,000 = 7,000 employees.

7. £35.10

EXPLANATION = £17.50 + £12.50 + £9.00 = £39. 10% = 10 ÷ 100 = 0.10. 0.10 × £39 = £3.90. £39 - £3.90 = £35.10

8. 60 grandparents and 90 parents

EXPLANATION = 2 + 3 = 5. 150 ÷ 5 = 30. 30 × 2 = 60. 3 × 30 = 90. Therefore, there are 60 grandparents and 90 parents at the play.

9. £43.80

EXPLANATION = 5 × £6.00 = £30.00. 3 × £4.60 = £13.80. £30 + £13.80 = £43.80

10. Tuesday

EXPLANATION = 13:00 + 32 hours = 9pm the next day.

11. 18 hours and 25 minutes

EXPLANATION = 08:45 to 14:30 = 5 hours and 45 minutes.

11:25 to 16:50 = 5 hours and 25 minutes.

16:00 to 23:15 = 6 hours and 15 minutes

Added together this equals = 18 hours and 25 minutes.

12. 1,065 people

EXPLANATION = 30% = 30 ÷ 100 = 0.30 × 3,550 = 1,065.

13. 8 sweets each

EXPLANATION = 32 ÷ 4 = 8

14. 4:2:1

EXPLANATION = The ratio is already in its simplest form, since there is only one orange ball.

15. £14.10

EXPLANATION = £70.50 ÷ 5 = £14.10

16. 1,080

EXPLANATION = 1 triangle = 180°. Therefore 6 triangles = 6 × 180° = 1,080°

17. 75

EXPLANATION = ¼ of 100 = 25. 100 − 25 = 75

18. £158.50

EXPLANATION = £23.50 × 3 = £70.50

£17.60 × 5 = £88

£70.50 + £88 = £158.50

19. 3:1

EXPLANATION = 45:15. To break down this ratio, you need to divide both numbers by the same figure. In this case, both can be divided by 15. $45 \div 15 = 3$. $15 \div 15 = 1$.

20. 18

EXPLANATION = $3 \times 6 = 18$

21. £9.00

EXPLANATION = $10\% = 10 \div 100 = 0.10$. $0.10 \times £10.00 = £1$. £10 - £1 = £9.

22. £80 per day

EXPLANATION = 7 days in a week. $£560 \div 7 = £80$.

23. 4:1

EXPLANATION = 20:5 – divide both by 5, to give a figure of 4:1.

24. £7.00

EXPLANATION =

$500 \times 1p = £5$ (100p in £1)

$100 \times 2p = £2$ ($50 \times 2p = £1$)

£5 + £2 = £7 total.

25. £560

EXPLANATION = $£7 \times 20 = £140$ per week.

$£140 \times 4 = £560$

NUMBERS EXERCISE 5

NUMBERS EXERCISE 5

Try to answer the questions quickly. You have 12 minutes in which to answer the 25 questions.

1. Polly draws 16 squares on a page. In total, how many degrees are there?

Answer

2. Melissa goes clothes shopping with £50 in her purse. How many tops could Melissa buy if each top was £8.50?

Answer

3. Joey had 150 sweets and he had to share them between himself and 5 other people. If Joey shared them equally, how many sweets would they have each?

Answer

4. A storm hit a town at approximately 2200 hours Monday night. The storm lasted for 16 hours. At what time did the storm end?

Answer

5. Rachel and two housemates went food shopping for the week. They split the cost between them. The food shopping came to £360.60. How much did each of them have to pay?

Answer

6. Dawn goes to the pet store. She buys 2 cats, 5 goldfish and 3 guinea pigs. A cat costs £16.50, a goldfish costs 80p and a guinea pig costs £6.80. In total, how much does Dawn spend?

Answer [   ]

7. Two companies merge together. One company has 8,880 employees and the other 4,560. Between both companies, they have to let go of 10% of employees. How many employees will be left?

Answer [   ]

8. Sophie has 8 times more awards than her best friend Claire. Sophie has 24. How many awards does Claire have?

Answer [   ]

9. Claire has 6 cats. She buys cat food every week. Each cat uses one tin of cat food per day. How many tins of cat food does Claire need to buy for one week?

Answer [   ]

10. A venue holds 18,000 spectators. The ratio of police to spectators must be 1:90. How many police would be needed if the venue was full?

Answer [   ]

11. Nathan has 40 basketball jerseys and he decides to give 25% of them to his nephew. How many jerseys is Nathan left with?

Answer [   ]

12. Sam wanted to buy the new England football kit for himself and his two children. The kits cost £46.99 for an adult size and £16.99 for a child size. In total, how much money would Sam have to spend if he were to buy the football kit for himself and his two children?

Answer [   ]

13. Adam is the coach of a football team. He wanted to buy himself and all the team new football shirts for the next match. There are 19 football players on his team excluding himself and each top would cost £17.50. If Adam receives a 20% discount on the total cost, how much would Adam have to pay?

Answer [   ]

14. A family of 4 all have jobs. Two members earn £150 a week and the other two members earn £75 a week. How much money does the whole family earn in a 4 week period?

Answer [   ]

15. Shaun has 500 marbles. He loses ¼ of them. How many marbles does Shaun have left?

Answer [   ]

16. Ella is going on holiday for two weeks. She wants to buy one swimsuit to wear for every day she is away. How many swimsuits will Ella need?

Answer

17. Four people are going on holiday. In total, the holiday costs £2,880. On average, how much money will each person have to pay?

Answer

18. Sally took 4 children to a play centre for the day. A children's pass costs £5.50 for the day. The policy of the day care is "pay for 2 children and 1 goes free". How much did it cost Sally to take her 4 children?

Answer

19. In a fish tank there are 12 white fish and 6 gold fish. What is the ratio of white to gold fish?

Answer

20. Ryan works 3 days a week and he earns £75 a day. How much money does Ryan earn if he works for 36 days?

Answer

21. Julie has 19 marbles. Her friends Justin and Tom have 36 marbles each. In total how many marbles do they have in total?

Answer

22. A library has 20,000 books on record per year. It is shown that each year 35% of books are not returned. How many books are not returned each year?

Answer [   ]

23. James buys a new suit. It is discounted at 20%. The suit costs £68.00. With the discount, how much does the suit cost James?

Answer [   ]

24. Andy has £10 and he decides to share his money between his 3 daughters. If Andy shares out the money equally, how much money would his 3 daughters each receive?

Answer [   ]

25. A beauty salon charges £12.50 for a half leg wax and £19.00 for a full leg wax. That day, the salon does 5 half leg waxes and 8 full leg waxes. How much money does the salon take that day?

Answer [   ]

ANSWERS TO NUMBERS EXERCISE 5

1. 5,760

EXPLANATION = 1 square = 360°. Therefore 16 squares = 360° × 16 = 5,760°

2. 5

EXPLANATION = £8.50 × 5 = £42.50. £8.50 × 6 = £51. Therefore the maximum number of tops that Melissa can buy is 5.

3. 25

EXPLANATION = 150 ÷ 6 = 25

4. 1400 on Tuesday

EXPLANATION = 22:00 + 16 hours = 14:00 on the following day.

5. £120.20

EXPLANATION = £360.60 ÷ 3 = £120.20

6. £57.40

EXPLANATION = 2 × £16.50 = £33

5 × 0.80 = £4

3 × £6.80 = £20.4

£33 + £4 + £20.40 = £57.40

7. 12,096

EXPLANATION = 8,880 + 4,560 = 13,440. 10% = 10 ÷ 100 = 0.10. 0.10 × 13,440 = 1,344. 13,440 − 1,344 = 12,096.

8. 3

EXPLANATION = 24 ÷ 8 = 3.

9. 42 tins of cat food

EXPLANATION = 6 tins per day, for 7 days = 42 tins per week.

10. 200

EXPLANATION = 18000 ÷ 90 = 200. 200 × 1 = 200.

11. 30

EXPLANATION = 25% = 25 ÷ 100 = 0.25. 0.25 × 40 = 10. 40 − 10 = 30.

12. £80.97

EXPLANATION = £16.99 × 2 = £33.98. £33.98 + £46.99 = £80.97

13. £280

EXPLANATION = 20 × £17.50 = £350. 20% = 20 ÷ 100 = 0.20. 0.20 × £350 = £70. £350 - £70 = £280.

14. £1,800

EXPLANATION = £150 × 2 = £300

£75 × 2 = £150

£300 + £150 = £450

£450 × 4 = £1,800

15. 375

EXPLANATION = ¼ of 500 = 125. 500 − 125 = 375

16. 14

EXPLANATION = Two weeks = 14 days, 1 swimsuit per day. Therefore Ella will need 14 swimsuits.

17. £720

EXPLANATION = £2,880 ÷ 4 = £720 per person.

18. £16.50

EXPLANATION = £5.50 × 2 = £11. This pays for 3 children (as the third goes free). There is still one child remaining, mean there will be an extra charge of £5.50 on top of the £11. £11 + £5.50 = £16.50

19. 2:1

EXPLANATION = 12:6 = 2:1

20. £2,700

EXPLANATION = £75 × 36 = £2,700

21. 91

EXPLANATION = 19 + 36 + 36 = 91

22. 7,000

EXPLANATION = 35% = 35 ÷ 100 = 0.35. 0.35 × 20,000 = 7,000.

23. £54.40

EXPLANATION = 20% = 20 ÷ 100 = 0.20. 0.20 × £68 = £13.60. £68 - £13.60 = £54.40

24. £3.33

EXPLANATION = £10 ÷ 3 = £3.33

25. £214.50

EXPLANATION = 5 × £12.50 = £62.50

8 × 19 = £152

£62.50 + £152 = £214.50

NUMBERS EXERCISE 6

NUMBERS EXERCISE 6

Try to answer the questions quickly. You have 12 minutes in which to answer the 25 questions.

1. A company goes into administration and they are selling all of their stock with a 60% discount. If a coat costs £45.00 at full price, how much would it cost with the 60% discount?

Answer [   ]

2. Martin buys some new holiday clothes. He buys a top costing £14.99, two pairs of shorts for £20 and a pair of sandals costing £8.50. He pays with a £50 note. How much change does Martin get?

Answer [   ]

3. Sam went to sleep at 10:30pm and he managed to get exactly 8 and half hours sleep. What time did Sam wake up?

Answer [   ]

4. Jack has 40 magic beans. He plants ¾ of them. How many magic beans does Jack have left?

Answer [   ]

5. If a concert starts at 9:15pm and it lasts for 9 hours, what time does the concert finish?

Answer [   ]

6. January has 31 days. That month, Jane received £1,085 bonus from work. On average, how much did Jane get for each day of the month?

Answer [   ]

7. Tom finishes school at 3.15pm and he must be home by 7pm. How long does Tom have out before he has to be home?

Answer [   ]

8. A teacher has 28 English papers to mark for her class. Each paper will take 9 minutes to mark. How long in hours and minutes will the teacher spend marking the papers?

Answer [   ]

9. A father goes into a shop to buy new pairs of trainers for each of his 3 children. He has £100 to spend. If he were to equally split the money between the 3 children, what is the maximum amount he could spend on each of his children's trainers?

Answer [   ]

10. Harry goes into a video store where each video costs £6.50. If he has £50 on his possession, how many videos can he buy?

Answer [   ]

11. A student needs to buy 5 books for their university course and they have £35.00 on their possession. If each book costs £4.50, how many books can the student buy?

Answer [ ]

12. A grandmother goes into a shop and spends £160. How much does she have to pay if she uses her 15% discount card?

Answer [ ]

13. A museum has 60 classic items. They are giving away a ¼ of these classic items to auction. How many items do they have to give away?

Answer [ ]

14. Sarah goes to see a musical in the west end. The show lasts for 3 hours and has a 45 minute break half way through. If the show starts at 5:45pm, what time will the show finish?

Answer [ ]

15. A CD store holds up to 15,000 CDs and 15% of these are rock and roll. How many CDs are rock and roll?

Answer [ ]

16. Mia has 12 times as many cousins as her friend Sophie. If Mia has 36 cousins, how many cousins does Sophie have?

Answer [ ]

17. Michael spent £160 in one shop and £95.50 in another. How much money did Michael spend altogether?

Answer [   ]

18. A royal parade was taking place midday on Sunday. The road was shut from 2100 Saturday night and opened again at 2200 on Sunday night. How many hours was the road shut for?

Answer [   ]

19. On average, if a police officer arrested 112 people in 4 weeks, how many people did he arrest a day?

Answer [   ]

20. The ambulance service received a call at 1300 hours. Due to a traffic jam, it took them 150 minutes to reach the scene. What time did they arrive at the scene?

Answer [   ]

21. A pregnant woman was expecting her baby on the 1st May. The baby arrived 18 days early. What date was the baby born?

Answer [   ]

22. If a concert ticket costs £25.60 and a group of 11 people went, how much in total would the group spend on tickets?

Answer [   ]

23. A family goes through a carton of milk a day. A carton of milk costs £1.55. If the family were to buy their milk for the next 8 days, how much would they spend?

Answer [   ]

24. A family of four went to a restaurant for dinner. Each course was £7.50 and each person had two courses in total. How much did the entire meal cost?

Answer [   ]

25. A family of 6 split the cost of all the household bills. The water bill was £70.80, the gas bill was £20.00 and the electric bill was £35.00, the rent for the month is £540. How much does each member of the family put towards covering the bill costs?

Answer [   ]

ANSWERS TO NUMBERS EXERCISE 6

1. £18.00

EXPLANATION = 60% = 60 ÷ 100 = 0.60 × £45 = £27. £45 - £27 = £18

2. £6.51

EXPLANATION = £14.99 + £20 + £8.50 = £43.49. £50 − £43.49 = £6.51

3. 7:00 am

EXPLANATION = 10:30 pm + 8 hours and 30 minutes = 7 am.

4. 10

EXPLANATION = ¾ of 40 = 30. 40 − 30 = 10.

5. 6:15 am

EXPLANATION = 9:15 pm + 9 hours = 6:15 am

6. £35

EXPLANATION = £1,085 ÷ 31 = £35

7. 3 hours and 45 minutes

EXPLANATION = 3:15 to 7 pm = 3 hours and 45 minutes

8. 4 hours and 12 minutes

EXPLANATION = 28 × 9 minutes = 252 minutes. 252 minutes = 4 hours and 12 minutes

9. £33.33

EXPLANATION = £100 ÷ 3 = £33.33

10. 7

EXPLANATION = £6.50 × 7 = £45.50. £6.50 × 8 = £52. Therefore, the maximum number of videos that Harry can buy is 7.

11. £12.50

EXPLANATION = £4.50 × 5 = £22.50. £35 – £22.50 = £12.50

12. £136

EXPLANATION = 15% = 15 ÷ 100 = 0.15. 0.15 × £160 = £24. £160 - £24 = £136

13. 15

EXPLANATION = ¼ of 60 = 15. 60 – 15 = 45

14. 9:30 pm

EXPLANATION = 5:45 pm + 3 hours and 45 minutes = 9.30 pm

15. 2,250

EXPLANATION = 15% = 15 ÷ 100 = 0.15. 0.15 × 15,000 = 2,250

16. 3

EXPLANATION = 36 ÷ 12 = 3

17. £255.50

EXPLANATION = £160 + £95.50 = £255.50

18. 25 hours

EXPLANATION = 21:00 Saturday, till 22:00 Sunday = 25 hours.

19. 4 people a day

EXPLANATION = 1 week = 7 days. Therefore, 4 weeks = 28 days (7 × 4). 112 ÷ 28 = 4

20. 15:30 pm

EXPLANATION = 150 minutes = 2 hours + 30 minutes. 13:00 pm + 2 hours and 30 minutes = 15:30 pm.

21. 13th of April

EXPLANATION = 1st May − 18 days = 13th April.

22. £281.60

EXPLANATION = £25.60 × 11 = £281.60

23. £12.40

EXPLANATION = £1.55 × 8 = £12.40

24. £60

EXPLANATION = 2 courses each, for 4 people = 8 courses in total. 8 × £7.50 = £60 in total for all of the courses together

25. £110.97

EXPLANATION = £70.80 + £20 + £35 + £540 = £665.80. £665.80 ÷ 6 = £110.97

NUMBERS EXERCISE 7

NUMBERS EXERCISE 7

Try to answer the questions quickly. You have 25 minutes in which to answer the 25 questions.

1. A cruise ship has 13 rows of windows. If each row has 39 windows, how many windows are there in total?

Answer [   ]

2. In a car park there are 325 cars, and each car has 4 tyres and 1 spare tyre. How many tyres are there throughout the car park?

Answer [   ]

3. A greengrocer has a box of 360 strawberries. The greengrocer wants to make up punnets of strawberries, each with 36 strawberries in it. How many punnets of strawberries can the greengrocer make?

Answer [   ]

4. A ball of wool measures 3.3 metres. If you have 100 balls of wool, how many metres will there be?

Answer [   ]

5. How many pieces of string measuring 1.25 metres in length can be cut from a ball which is 100m long?

Answer [   ]

6. One case containing 42 cartons of orange juice costs £6.30. How much will two cartons of orange juice cost?

Answer

7. A moped is travelling at a speed of 35 mph. How long does it take to travel 7 miles?

Answer

8. A train travels a total distance of 540 miles at a constant speed of 90 mph. How long does the journey last?

Answer

9. What speed do you need to travel to go 100 miles in 2 hours?

Answer

10. A prisoner has escaped from prison. The prison is 20 miles away. You need to get there in 15 minutes. How fast do you need to drive?

Answer

11. A CD album has 49 minutes worth of songs. If each song is 3 minutes 30 seconds long, how many songs are on the album?

Answer

12. A coach driver is making a journey from Land's End to John O'Groats. This is a distance of 420 miles. He has to make 7 equal stops. How many miles apart does each stop have to be?

Answer [   ]

13. A train has 6 trams and each tram holds 80 tonnes of freight. What is the total weight of freight carried by the train?

Answer [   ]

14. An office has 333 computer desks. If only 2/3 are used, how many are un-used?

Answer [   ]

15. Mike cycles every day for 30 minutes. How much time does he spend cycling over 8 days?

Answer [   ]

16. A rugby club raises its annual subscription of £300 by 25%. What will the new subscription be?

Answer [   ]

17. A cinema ticket costs £5.00. If a pensioner is given a 15% discount, how much change will they get from a £20 note?

Answer [   ]

18. A circle has a diameter of 240 mm. What is the length, in centimetres, of the radius?

Answer [ ]

19. Below is a bar chart showing yearly vegetable sales for a market in Castleton. What is the average yearly sale of mushrooms over the three years?

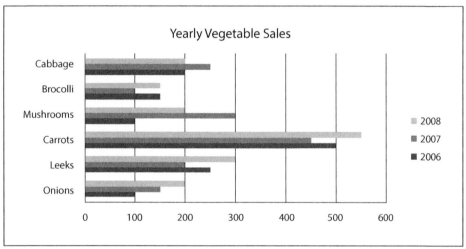

Answer [ ]

20. Roger needs to lay new turf in his garden. The whole of the garden will need new turf. Calculate the area of the garden that will need new turf.

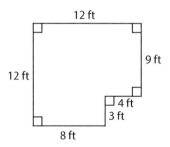

Answer [ ]

21. If I have £40 in my wallet and spend £13.75 of it, how much will I have left?

Answer

22. A motorist is travelling at 80 mph. How far will he have travelled in 15 minutes?

Answer

23. A prison cell holds two people. There are two prison areas: high risk and low risk. The high risk area has 123 cells and the low risk area has 334 cells. How many prisoners are there in the prison?

Answer

24. A food processing company has 10 people a week absent due to illness. How many people are absent due to illness in a year?

Answer

25. Balmoray Police operates a three-shift working pattern in each day. Each shift has to have 22 police officers on duty. How many officers are required for a day's work?

Answer

ANSWERS TO NUMBERS EXERCISE 7

1. 507

EXPLANATION = $13 \times 39 = 507$. Therefore there are 507 windows in total.

2. 1,625

EXPLANATION = If each car has 4 tyres and 1 spare tyre, then each car has 5 tyres total. 325 cars with 5 tyres total = 1,625 tyres overall.

3. 10

EXPLANATION = $36 \times 10 = 360$. Therefore, the greengrocer can make exactly 10 punnets of 36, with 360 strawberries.

4. 330 metres

EXPLANATION = $100 \times 3.3 = 330$ metres of wool in total.

5. 80

EXPLANATION = $100 / 1.25 = 80$. Therefore, you can cut 80 pieces of 1.25 m string, from a 100 m ball.

6. 30 p

EXPLANATION = To work out this question you need to establish the cost of individual cartons of orange juice. £6.30 / 0.42 = 15. Therefore, the price for one carton of orange juice is £0.15. This means that two cartons of orange juice will cost £0.30, or 30 p.

7. 12 minutes

EXPLANATION = You need to divide the distance by the speed. So 7 / 35 = 0.2.

0.2 of an hour = 12 minutes.

8. 360 minutes

EXPLANATION = Simply divide the distance by the speed. 540 / 90 = 6. 6 hours = 360 minutes.

9. 50 mph

EXPLANATION = If you go 100 miles in 2 hours, then you will go 50 miles in one hour, assuming you are moving at a constant speed.

10. 80 mph

EXPLANATION = 15 minutes = 0.25 of an hour. Divide 20 by 0.25 to reach the answer = 80 mph.

11. 14

EXPLANATION = In order to work this out, you need to put the minutes into seconds. 49 minutes = 2,940 seconds. 3 minutes 30 seconds = 210 seconds total. So, 2,940 ÷ 210 = 14

12. 60

EXPLANATION = If the coach driver is travelling 420 miles, and making 7 equal stops, then the stops will need to be 60 miles apart. 420 / 7 = 60.

13. 480 tonnes

EXPLANATION = 6 × 80 = 480 tonnes

14. 111

EXPLANATION = 2/3 of 333 = 222. 333 − 222 = 111

15. 4 hours

EXPLANATION = 30 minutes × 8 = 240 minutes. 240 minutes = 4 hours.

16. £375

EXPLANATION = £300 × 25% = 300 × 0.25 = £75. £300 + £75 = £375.

17. £15.75

EXPLANATION = 15% of £5 = 5 × 0.15 = 0.75. £5 − £0.75 = £4.25. So, the cost for the ticket will be £4.25. £20 − £4.25 = £15.75 change

18. 12 cm

EXPLANATION = 240 mm = 24 cm. The radius = half the length of the circle, meaning the radius of the circle is 12 cm.

19. 200

EXPLANATION = 200 + 300 + 100 = 600. 600 ÷ 3 (years) = 200.

20. 132 ft²

EXPLANATION = Divide the turf into two squares, and then work out the area of each. So, on the left hand square work out 12 ft × 8 ft = 96 ft², then on the right hand square work out 9 ft × 4 ft = 36 ft². Then add 96 ft² to 36 ft², to get 132 ft².

21. £26.25

EXPLANATION = £40 − £13.75 = £26.25

22. 20 miles

EXPLANATION = 15 minutes = 0.25 of an hour. 80 × 0.25 = 20.

23. 914

EXPLANATION = 123 × 2 = 246. 334 × 2 = 668. 668 + 246 = 914

24. 520

EXPLANATION = There are 52 weeks in a year. 10 × 52 = 520

25. 66

EXPLANATION = If there are three-shift patterns, consisting of 22 officers per time, then the answer is 22 × 3 = 66 officers per day.

NUMBERS EXERCISE 8

NUMBERS EXERCISE 8

Try to answer the questions quickly. You have 25 minutes in which to answer the 25 questions.

1. In the Johnson family there are 7 people; 3 of them are female. What is this as a fraction?

Answer [   ]

2. You are at a traffic collision in Glasgow where a vehicle has crashed into a play area. As part of your documentation you need to calculate the area of the playing field. Using the diagram below, work out the area of the playing field and select the appropriate answer.

Answer [   ]

3. Your yearly salary is £40,000. You also receive a yearly bonus which is 15% of your salary. How much do you earn per year?

Answer [   ]

4. On a housing estate in Edinburgh there are 34,000 homes. Of these homes 63% are semi-detached, 30% are detached, and the remainder are terraced houses. How many houses are terraced?

Answer [   ]

5. You have two foot patrols a day. The total distance walked is 20 miles. If you walked at an average speed of 4 mph, how long is each patrol?

Answer

6. You are tasked to drive your boss to a meeting 100 miles away. You will be driving at 60 mph. If you set off at 10:20pm, what time would you arrive?

Answer

7. A criminal sprints at a speed of 10 metres every 2 seconds. How long does it take him to run 1,000 metres if he continues at the same speed?

Answer

8. You are at a fruit and vegetable stall at a market. If one apple costs 41p, how much would it cost to buy 11 apples?

Answer

9. A car garage orders four new sport cars costing £41,000 each. How much in total has the garage spent on the new sports cars?

Answer

10. A water tank has a maximum capacity of 200 litres. If the tank is 80% full, how many more litres are required to fill it to its maximum?

Answer

11. If I spend £1.60, £2.35, £3.55 and £4.75 on a selection of goods, how much will I have spent in total?

Answer [   ]

12. Below is a chart showing snowfall across the Lincolnshire region in 2004 in centimetres. What is the combined snowfall for January and May?

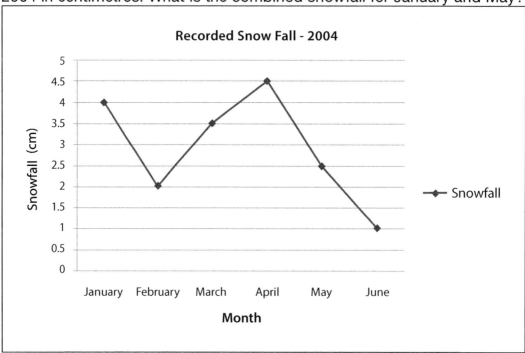

Answer [   ]

13. On Monday it takes Lucy 52 minutes to get to work. On Tuesday it takes 40 minutes, Wednesday takes 51 minutes, on Thursday it takes 1 hour 2 minutes and on Friday it takes 1 hour 30 minutes. How long did her average commute take?

Answer [   ]

14. Paul is a 100 metre sprinter. During a weekend-long competition he runs the distance in 11 seconds, 9 seconds, 9.5 seconds and 11.5 seconds. What is the average time that Paul runs 100 metres in?

Answer [   ]

15. One in fourteen people become a victim of car crime each year. In Saxby there are 224 people. On that basis, how many people per year experience car crime in Saxby?

Answer [   ]

16. Lisa's weekly newspaper bill is £5.50 and the delivery charge is 35 p per week. How much does she have to pay over six weeks?

Answer [   ]

17. A gardener wants to gravel over the area shown below. One bag of gravel will cover 20 m². How many bags are needed to cover the entire garden?

10 m
50 m
40 m
20 m

Answer [   ]

18. The gardener decides he is only going to gravel 20% of the garden. Using the above diagram, how many square metres will he be gravelling?

Answer [   ]

19. You stop and search 40 people, and 8 of them are arrested for possession of a class A drug. What is this as a fraction in it's simplest form?

Answer [   ]

20. There are 144 people entered into a raffle, 12 people each win a prize. What is this as a fraction in it's simplest form?

Answer [   ]

21. At a music festival there are 35,000 festival goers, 5% of these are under 16 years of age. How many festival goers were under 16?

Answer [   ]

22. At Christmas you buy 30 presents; 12 are bought for your family and 18 for your friends. What percentage was bought for your friends?

Answer [   ]

23. Over one year, PC Smith files details of 600 drink driving cases. These are divided into 5 piles dependant upon how over the limit the drink driver was. If the piles are all equal sizes, how many are in each pile?

Answer [   ]

24. On average, 1 out of every 30 people experience back problems in their lifetime. Out of 900 people, how many will experience back problems?

Answer [   ]

25. Below are a toy company's monthly sale figures. Calculate the average toy sales per month for the year.

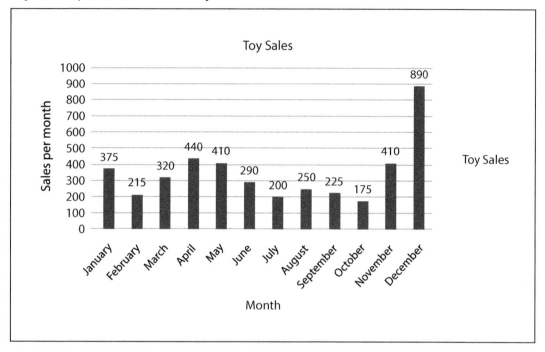

Answer [   ]

ANSWERS TO NUMBERS EXERCISE 8

1. 3/7

EXPLANATION = 3/7 is the final fraction and cannot be simplified. There are 3 females out of 7 total family members.

2. 900 m²

Add the two areas together: 20 m × 45 m = 900. 10 m × 20 m = 200. 900 + 200 = 1,100. Then minus the 200 from the top of the diagram, to give you the area of just the playing field.

3. £46,000

EXPLANATION = 15% of £40,000 = 40,000 × 0.15 = 6,000. £40,000 + £6,000 = £46,000

4. 2,380

EXPLANATION = 63% + 30% = 93%, meaning that there is the 7% left – all of which are terraced houses. 7% of 34,000 = 2,380

5. 2 hours and 30 minutes

EXPLANATION = To work this out, divide the distance by the speed. 20 ÷ 4 = 5. 5 hours. 5 hours divided by 2 (for two patrols) = 2 hours and 30 minutes.

6. 12 am

EXPLANATION = 60 miles = 60 minutes, therefore 120 miles = 120 minutes. We are travelling at 20 miles every 20 minutes, meaning it would take 1 hour and 40 minutes to go 100 miles. If we set off at 10:20 pm, we would arrive within 1 hour and 40 minutes. This means we'd arrive at 12:00 am.

7. 200 seconds

EXPLANATION = To work out the answer, simply do distance divided by speed, so 1,000 ÷ 5 metres per second, which gives you 200.

8. £4.51

EXPLANATION = 41p × 11 = £4.51

9. £164,000

EXPLANATION = £41,000 × 4 = £164,000

0. 40 litres

EXPLANATION = 80% of 200 = 160. 200 − 160 = 40 litres.

1. £12.25

EXPLANATION = £1.60+ £2.35 + £3.55 + £4.75 = £12.25

2. 6.5 cm

EXPLANATION = There were 4 cm of snow in January, and 2.5 cm of snow in May.

3. 59 minutes

EXPLANATION = 52 minutes + 40 minutes + 51 minutes + 62 minutes + 90 minutes = 295 / 5 = 59 minutes

4. 10.25 seconds

EXPLANATION = 11 + 9 + 9.5 + 11.5 = 41 /4 = 10.25

5. 16

EXPLANATION = (1/14) × 224 = 16 people.

6. £35.10

EXPLANATION = £5.50 + £0.35 = £5.85. £5.85 × 6 = £35.10

7. 75

EXPLANATION = Cut the two blocks in half. Then you have 10 m × 50 m = 500 m. 20 m x 50 m = 1,000m. 1,000 + 500 = 1,500 m. 1,500/20 = 75 bags.

8. 300 m²

EXPLANATION = 20% of 1,500 m = 300.

9. 1/5

EXPLANATION = 8/40 simplified = 1/5

20. 1/12

EXPLANATION = 12/144 = 1/12

21. 1,750

EXPLANATION = 5% of 35,000 = 1,750

22. 60%

EXPLANATION = 18/30 = 0.60

0.60 × 100 = 60%

23. 120

EXPLANATION = 600/5 = 120 files

24. 30

EXPLANATION = 1/30 = 0.033

0.033 × 900 = 30

25. 350

EXPLANATION = 375 + 215 + 320 + 440 + 410 + 290 + 200 + 250 + 225 + 175 + 410 + 890 = 4,200.

4,200 ÷ 12 = 350.

BETTERING YOUR MATHEMATICS

Now that we've provided you with some of the basics for your Scottish Police Numbers Test, we think it is important that you put these skills to the ultimate test.

The purpose of this section is to enhance your knowledge regarding maths. Although the questions in this section might not replicate the ones in your actual assessment, they are a great way to learn how to use those techniques in more challenging questions.

It's important that you are able to answer questions no matter the format or question type. In order to see how well you are getting on, have a go at these practice questions.

These questions are designed to be challenging, so if you get stuck, be sure to check out the answer section.

We have not provided a time limit for this section. Work through this section at your own pace and improve your mathematical learning!

Representation of the grades students achieved across five subjects

	English	Maths	Science	History	Media
David	A-	B+	C-	C+	B+
Billy	C-	C+	B+	A+	A
Elliott	B+	B-	A+	A-	C
Taralyn	C+	B+	B+	C+	A+
Alecia	C	C+	A-	B-	C+
James	B-	B+	C-	C+	C
Gareth	B+	B-	A	B-	C-
Duncan	B-	C-	C+	C-	C
Joe	B+	B	B	C	A

Grade	Pass Mark
A+	96-100
A	91-95
A-	86-90
B+	81-85
B	76-80
B-	71-75
C+	65-70
C	59-64
C-	50-58

1. In the above table, find the minimum possible total marks for all nine candidates in Science.

A	B	C	D	E
507	776	667	676	None of these

2. In the above table, what is the highest total mark across all five subjects that David could have got?

A	B	C	D	E
298	386	320	408	None of these

3. There are two lists of numbers. One list contains 11 numbers, the average of which is 36. The second list contains 13 numbers and has the average of 41. If the two lists are combined, what is the average of the numbers in the new list? To the nearest whole number.

A	B	C	D	E
36	37	38	39	40

4. The diagram below shows the plan of a building site. All angles are right angles.

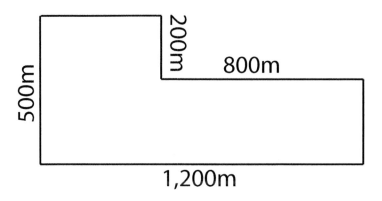

What is the area of the building site? Give your answer in hectares.

1 hectare = 10,000 m² = 2.47 acres.

A	B	C	D
60 hectares	40 hectares	44 hectares	4.4 hectares

5. The diagram below shows the layout of an animal sanctuary.

The animal sanctuary contains 6 separate enclosures for different animals.

The animal sanctuary is a rectangle with the following dimensions:

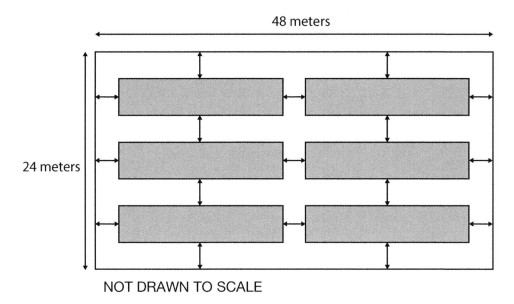

NOT DRAWN TO SCALE

The distance from the outer edge of the sanctuary to the enclosures must be 1.5 metres.

The distance between each enclosure must be 1.5 metres.

Each enclosure is the exact same size. Using the information provided in the diagram above, work out the length and height of an enclosure.

Length

Height

Carbon Emissions

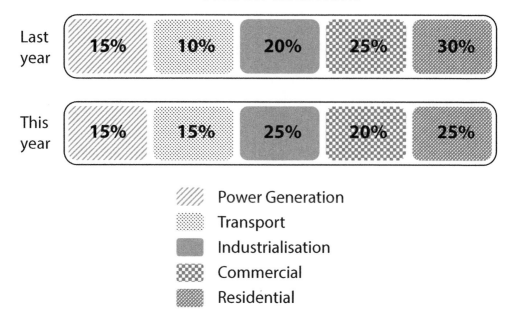

Last year	15%	10%	20%	25%	30%

Power Generation
Transport
Industrialisation
Commercial
Residential

6. If transport emitted 6 million tons this year, and industrial emissions are the same as last year, what were the commercial emissions last year?

A	B	C	D	E
11.5 million tons	10 million tons	3 million tons	12.5 million tons	8.5 million tons

7. A square field, S, has an area greater than 6400m2. Its length is increased by 31m and its width is also increased by 35m to give a rectangular field, R. Which one out of the following is true?

A. Area S > area R and perimeter S > perimeter R

B. Area S = area R and perimeter S = perimeter R

C. Area S < area R and perimeter S < perimeter R

D. Area S < area R and perimeter S > perimeter R

E. Area S > area R and perimeter S = perimeter R

Answer

8. A bank pays 6.8% compound interest per year on an investment of £7,000.

What is the value of the investment after two years? Round your answer to 2 decimal places.

Answer

9. The following table shows the cost of booking holidays from a travel agent for next year.

HOLIDAY PRICES				
Types of Holiday Deals	Turkey	Mexico	America	Spain
All inclusive	£276pp	£720pp	£880pp	£320pp
Half board	£220pp	£640pp	£795pp	£275pp
Self-Catering	£180pp	£550pp	£620pp	£235pp

Work out the difference in cost of booking three all-inclusive holidays to Mexico, for two people, instead of booking one-self-catering holiday to Turkey for five people.

A	B	C	D
£1,250	£3,420	£9,000	£4,500

10. Kent Police have put out a tender for electrical equipment and supplies. Below are quotes from 3 suppliers.

Electrical Equipment and Supplies	Supplier 1 Total cost over 2 years (£)	Supplier 2 Total cost over 2 years (£)	Supplier 3 Total cost over 1 years (£)
Basic Services	34,550	36,660	15,450
Electrical Safety Checks	39,550	42,000	20,000
Full Equipment Maintenance	120,850	150,500	60,000

Based on an annual year cost, which supplier offers the best price for electrical safety checks?

A	B	C	D
Supplier 1	Supplier 2	Supplier 3	All the same

11. Study the following graph carefully and answer the questions given below.

This graph shows the distribution of candidates who were enrolled for a fitness course and the candidates (out of those enrolled) who passed the course in different institutes.

Candidates enrolled = 1500

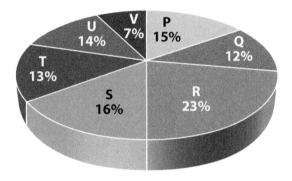

Candidates passed = 920

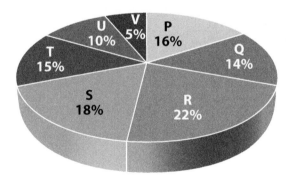

Which institute has the highest percentage of candidates passing the selection process to candidates enrolled?

A	B	C	D
Institute P	Institute Q	Institute T	Institute V

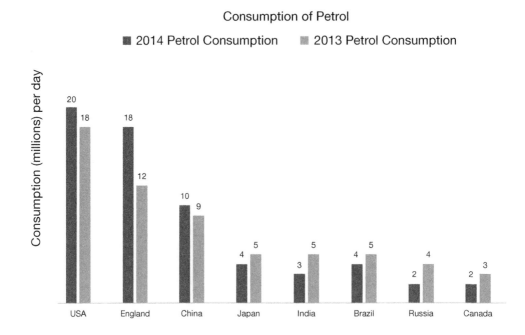

Consumption of Petrol

■ 2014 Petrol Consumption   ■ 2013 Petrol Consumption

12. In England, if the petrol consumption per year continued to rise by 6.8% until 2016 and then decreased by 4% from 2016 to 2018, what would be the petrol consumption per day in 2018?

A	B	C	D
18.9 million	19 million	21.5 million	19.8 million

13. The set of data below shows the results in a year 11 Media mock exam. The marks are out of 100%. The teacher wants to find the mean mark for this test which was given to 68 pupils. Give your answer to 1 decimal place.

Media mock exam (%)	No. of pupils	No. of pupils X media mock exam (%)
10	0	$10 \times 0 = 0$
20	2	$20 \times 2 = 40$
30	3	
40	6	
50	8	
60	11	
70	8	
80	15	
90	12	
100	3	
Totals	68	

The mean mark is:

14. Look at the sequence below:

1   9   17   25   33   ...   ...

What are the next two terms in the sequence?

15. A sequence uses the following rule:

$$n^{th} \text{ term} = 3(n + 1)$$

Work out the first six terms in this sequence, using the rule provided. 'N' represents the term number in the sequence. Fill in the table below with your answers.

1st term	2nd term	3rd term	4th term	5th term	6th term

16. Factorise:

$$12 + 20x$$

17. Factorise:

$$x^2 - 81$$

18. Solve:

$$6(x - 3) = x + 7$$

19. Simplify:

$$a^2 + a^2$$

20. Factorise completely:

$$20a^2 - 10a$$

21.

(a) Circle the THREE squared numbers.

17 45 49 12 64 91 50 4 5 18 30 15

(b) Circle ALL of the factors of 90.

17 45 49 12 64 91 50 4 5 18 30 15

(c) Circle ALL of the prime numbers.

17 45 49 12 64 91 50 4 5 18 30 15

22. Here is a map of an island.

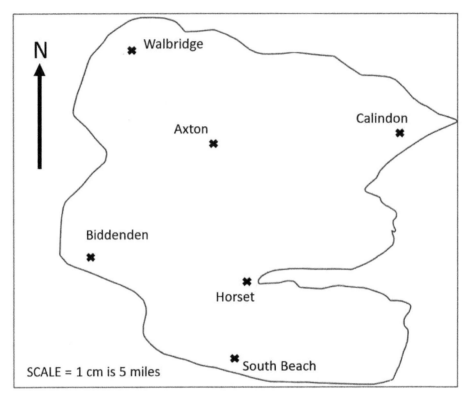

Write down the bearing from Calindon to Biddenden.

23. Write each of the following expressions in their simplest form.

(a) 8^0

(b) $9^9 \times 9^5$

(c) $7^8 \div 7^7$

(d) $13^9 \div 13^1$

(e) $y^{15} \times y^4$

24. Using trial and improvement, solve the equation $x^2 + 2x = 40$, correct to 1 decimal place.

25. Andy says that $4 \times 3 - 2 \times 7 = -2$

Ryan says the answer to this calculation is 70.

Who is correct, and explain your reasons why.

ANSWERS

Q1. D = 676

EXPLANATION = 50 + 81 + 96 + 81 + 86 + 50 + 91 + 65 + 76 = 676.

Q2. E = none

EXPLANATION = 90 + 85 + 58 + 70 + 85 = 388. None of the answers match, so therefore the answer must be 'none'.

Q3. D = 39

EXPLANATION = 11 × 36 = 396. 13 × 41 = 533. 533 + 396 = 929 ÷ (11 + 13) = 38.708. To the nearest whole number = 39.

Q4. C = 44 hectares

EXPLANATION = Work out the area of the whole shape: 1,200 × 500 = 600,000

Work out the area of the missing rectangle (to make a complete rectangle): 800 × 200 = 160,000

- So, 600,000 − 160,000 = 440,000 m².
- 440,000 m² in hectares = 440,000 ÷ 10,000 = 44 hectares.

Q5. Length of each enclosure = 21.75 metres
        Height of each enclosure = 6 metres

EXPLANATION = To work out the length = total 48 metres

- 48 − 1.5 − 1.5 − 1.5 = 43.5
- 43.5 ÷ 2 = 21.75 metres

To work out the height = total 24 metres

- 24 − 1.5 − 1.5 − 1.5 − 1.5 = 18
- 18 ÷ 3 = 6 metres

Q6. D = 12.5 million tons

EXPLANATION = if transport emissions this year are 6 million tons – and equal 15% of the total – the overall total for this year would be 6,000,000 × 100 ÷ 15% = 40,000,000.

So industrial emissions for this year would be = 40,000,000 ÷ 100 × 25 = 10,000,000.

The industrial emissions are the same for last year, so to work out the overall total of last year = 10,000,000 × 100 ÷ 20 = 50,000,000.

So the commercial emissions for last year = 50,000,000 ÷ 100 × 25 = 12,500,000 (12.5 million tons).

Q7. C = Area S < area R and perimeter S < perimeter R

EXPLANATION = if the perimeter is increased on both sides of the Square field S, that means the area of square field R is going to be bigger. This is also true about the perimeter; if both sides are increased in size to form field R, which means the perimeter for R is going to be bigger than that of perimeter S. So, the correct way to demonstrate this is answer C.

Q8. £7,984.37

EXPLANATION = for this question, it is vitally important to remember that interest will be added on to previous interest.

Step 1 = for the first year = 7,000 ÷ 100 × 6.8 = £476.

• So, 7,000 + 476 = 7,476.

Step 2 = for the second year = 7,476 ÷ 100 × 6.8 = £508.37.

• So, 7,476 + 508.37 = £7,984.37.

Q9. B = £3,420

EXPLANATION = Self-catering holiday to Turkey for 5 people = 180 × 5 = 900.

All-inclusive holiday to Mexico for 2 people = 720 × 2 = 1,440. Booked three times = 1,440 × 3 = 4,320.

• So, 4,320 – 900 = 3,420.

Q10. A = Supplier 1

EXPLANATION = Supplier 1 = 39,550 ÷ 2 = 19,775

Supplier 2 = 42,000 ÷ 2 = 21,000

Supplier 3 = 20,000

Therefore, Supplier 1 offers the best price for electrical safety checks, for one year.

Q11. B = Institute Q

EXPLANATION =

$$P = \left[\left(\frac{16\% \text{ of } 920}{15\% \text{ of } 1500}\right) \times 100\right]\% = \left[\frac{16 \times 920}{15 \times 1500} \times 100\right]\% = 65.42\%.$$

$$Q = \left[\left(\frac{14\% \text{ of } 920}{12\% \text{ of } 1500}\right) \times 100\right]\% = 71.56\%.$$

$$R = \left[\left(\frac{22\% \text{ of } 920}{23\% \text{ of } 1500}\right) \times 100\right]\% = 58.67\%.$$

$$S = \left[\left(\frac{18\% \text{ of } 920}{16\% \text{ of } 1500}\right) \times 100\right]\% = 69\%.$$

$$T = \left[\left(\frac{15\% \text{ of } 920}{13\% \text{ of } 1500}\right) \times 100\right]\% = 70.77\%.$$

$$U = \left[\left(\frac{10\% \text{ of } 920}{14\% \text{ of } 1500}\right) \times 100\right]\% = 43.81\%.$$

$$V = \left[\left(\frac{5\% \text{ of } 920}{7\% \text{ of } 1500}\right) \times 100\right]\% = 43.81\%.$$

So, the institute with the highest percentage rate of candidates passed, to candidates enrolled, is Institute Q.

Q12. A = 18.9 million

EXPLANATION = first, you need to work out the percentage increase each year from 2014 to 2016.

So, in 2014 there is 18 (million); to work out a 6.8% increase would equal 106.8%. So, 18 ÷ 100 × 106.8 = 19.2 (million). This is the consumption for 2015. From 2015 to 2016, the same thing applies. 19.2 ÷ 100 × 106.8% = 20.5 (million).

From 2016 to 2017, there is a 4% decrease. So, 20.5 ÷ 100 × 96% = 19.7 (million). From 2017 to 2018 = 19.7 ÷ 100 × 96% = 18.9 (million).

Q13. 67.2%

EXPLANATION = Add up the "number of pupils multiplied by media mock exam" and then divide it by the "number of pupils".

Media mock exam (%)	No. of pupils	No. of pupils X media mock exam (%)
10	0	10 × 0 = 0
20	2	20 × 2 = 40
30	3	30 × 3 =90
40	6	40 × 6 = 240
50	8	50 × 8 = 400
60	11	60 × 11 = 660
70	8	70 × 8 = 560
80	15	80 × 15 = 1,200
90	12	90 × 12 = 1,080
100	3	100 × 3 = 300
Totals	67	4,570

So, 4,570 ÷ 68 = 67.2%.

Q14. 41 and 49

EXPLANATION = The number sequence is adding 8 to the previous number.

Q15. Your answer should look like this:

1st term	2nd term	3rd term	4th term	5th term	6th term
6	9	12	15	18	21

Q16. $4 (3 + 5x)$

Q17. $(x + 9) (x - 9)$

Q18. $x = 5$

- $6x - 18 = x + 7$
- $5x - 18 = 7$
- $5x = 25$
- $x = 5$

-

Q19. $2a^2$

- $a + a = 2a$
- Both of these are being squared, so $2a$ squared $= 2a^2$.

Q20. $10a (2a - 1)$

- Highest common factor $= 10$
- $10a (2a - 1)$
- $= 20a^2 - 10a$

Q21. (a) 49, 64 and 4

- $2 \times 2 = 4$
- $7 \times 7 = 49$
- $8 \times 8 = 64$

Q21. (b) 45, 5, 18, 30, 15

EXPLANATION = The factors of 90 are:

- 1 and 90;
- 2 and 45;
- 3 and 30;
- 5 and 18;
- 6 and 15;
- 9 and 10.

Q21. (c) 17 and 5

EXPLANATION = Prime numbers are numbers that can only be divided by itself and one:

- $1 \times 17 = 17$ (no other numbers can be divided into 17).
- $1 \times 5 = 5$ (no other numbers can be divided into 5).

Q22. 249°

- The bearing from Calindon to Biddenden is 249°.

Q23. (a) 1

Q23. (b) 9^{14}

- $9^9 \times 9^5 = 9^{9+5}$

Q23. (c) 7^1 or 7

- $7^8 \div 7^7 = 7^{8-7}$

Q23. (d) 13^8

- $13^9 \div 13^1 = 13^{9-1}$

Q23 (e) y^{19}

- $y^{15} \times y^4 = y^{15+4}$

Q24. $x = 5.4$

Let's start with $y = 5$

- $5 \times 5 = 25$

- $2 \times 5 = 10$

- $25 + 10 = 35$ TOO SMALL

Let's try with $y = 6$

- $6 \times 6 = 36$

- $2 \times 6 = 12$

- $36 + 12 = 48$ TOO BIG

Let's try with $y = 5.5$

- $5.5 \times 5.5 = 30.25$

- $2 \times 5.5 = 11$

- $30.25 + 11 = 41.25$ TOO BIG

Let's try with $y = 5.4$

- $5.4 \times 5.4 = 29.16$

- $2 \times 5.4 = 10.8$

- $29.16 + 10.8 = 39.96$ CLOSE

Therefore correct to 1 decimal place = 5.4

Q25. Andy is correct. You need to do the multiplications before subtraction (BIDMAS).

- $4 \times 3 = 12$
- $2 \times 7 = 14$
- $12 - 14 = -2$

A FEW FINAL WORDS

You have now reached the end of the testing guide and no doubt you will be ready to take the numbers test element of the Scottish Police Test.

The majority of candidates who pass the police officer selection process have a number of common attributes. These are as follows:

1. They believe in themselves.

The first factor is self-belief. Regardless of what anyone tells you, you can become a police officer. Just like any job of this nature, you have to be prepared to work hard in order to be successful. Make sure you have the self-belief to pass the selection process and fill your mind with positive thoughts.

2. They prepare fully.

The second factor is preparation. Those people who achieve in life prepare fully for every eventuality and that is what you must do when you apply to become a police officer. Work very hard and especially concentrate on your weak areas.

3. They persevere.

Perseverance is a fantastic word. Everybody comes across obstacles or setbacks in their life, but it is what you do about those setbacks that is important. If you fail at something, then ask yourself 'why' you have failed. This will allow you to improve for next time and if you keep improving and trying, success will eventually follow. Apply this same method of thinking when you apply to become a police officer.

4. They are self-motivated.

How much do you want this job? Do you want it, or do you *really* want it?

When you apply to join the police you should want it more than anything in the world. Your levels of self-motivation will shine through on your application and during your interview. For the weeks and months leading up to the police officer selection process, be motivated as best you can and always keep your fitness levels up as this will serve to increase your levels of motivation.

Work hard, stay focused and be what you want…

The How2Become Team

P.S. Don't forget, you can get FREE access to more tests online at:

www.PsychometricTestsOnline.co.uk

NEED A LITTLE EXTRA HELP?

PASS YOUR SCOTTISH POLICE ASSESSMENTS

FOR MORE INFORMATION ON OUR SCOTTISH POLICE GUIDES, PLEASE VISIT

WWW.HOW2BECOME.COM

Get Access To
FREE
Psychometric
Tests

www.PsychometricTestsOnline.co.uk

Printed in Great
Britain
by Amazon